Time

To

Quit?

The questions you need to be
asking about your career.

Wick Kaminski

Paperback ISBN-13: 978-1983126611

CONTENTS

---

[1] Numbering is dumb, right?

DEDICATION

For his wildly indirect, chaotic, and beautiful lessons that brought me to realize that I truly do have the freedom to be whatever I want to be and create whatever I want to create, I have to dedicate this to my dad. To my dad for believing in me, and for doing everything in his power to set me up for success—even if we butted heads over it constantly. To my dad who I am slowly becoming, which scares the shit out of me every single day.

Love you.

START HERE

You've heard the story a million times:

Follow your passion and you'll never work a day in your life.

And if you're reading this book, you're someone who wonders all the time:

How the fuck am I supposed to know what my passion is?
And how the fuck will I know when I've found it?

Don't worry. We all do. It's okay. I'm here to help.

THE POINT

You are someone who's unclear about whether or not you're getting satisfaction from your job. If you weren't, we wouldn't be talking right now. You're seeking a greater sense of being through your work, either where you're at now or in thinking about potential new futures. The purpose of this book is to help you be honest and vulnerable with yourself about which side of the fence you're actually leaning towards. I want you to leave this book either realizing that you're actually crushing it and enjoying your job, or realizing that it might be a good time for you to consider other pathways in your life.

You need to read this book because it's a challenge. You may not need it today, you may not need it a year from now, but at some point in your career this book is going to become an important tool for you.

Maybe you're a millennial just finishing up your first year at your first job after graduating school and you're having those moments of "holy shit this is my life now" and "I don't think I want to do this forever." You probably find it frustrating that all

3

these influencers and marketing campaigns are telling you to #liveauthentic because you seriously doubt the validity of their platforms but still somehow they make you question whether you actually *could* be living more #authentically.

Maybe you're in your fifties, decades into your career, and feeling like it never really clicked for you. Maybe you're somewhere in the middle. Maybe you're still figuring it out. This book is for you, too.

I'm not here to answer the question of *what* your passion is. But I'm here to help you realize that there might actually be a path to figuring it out. And depending on your situation, my questions might help you realize that you're on the right path already, or it might end up being the first step toward getting you there. Either way, it should give you a better idea of where you stand along your career path.

Let me be clear. The point of this book is *not* to make you quit your job. The point of this book is to give you the tools to reflect critically on the fulfillment that your work supplies to your overall life, create clear, direct communication about your goals and ambitions, and help you demand the excellence and growth you deserve from your work/life harmony.

To set the context for the coming chapters and the main focus of this book, let me share a quick story about some terrible advice and an existential crisis.

PROLOGUE

Stop telling me to follow my passion.

'Twas a dark and stormy Tuesday night in the city of
Costa Mesa, right in the heart of Orange County in
Southern California. Usually Tuesday night meant one
thing—gathering the crew after work for frisbee in
the park before hitting Taco Tuesday at one of the
favorite neighborhood spots for a wave of carne
asada goodness. But this Tuesday was different. In
lieu of the usual Taco Tuesday routine, I had instead
opted to attend a small, private networking event for
alumni from my university.

I was two years out of college, and two years into my
first real job. And after two years of facilitating online
sales of tasty gift sets, I was at this networking event
because I had decided that it was time to leave my
job, change industries, move to Silicon Valley, and
start my career in the technology sector. More
specifically, I had spent months struggling through
the natural quarter-life existential crisis that arises
after entering the workforce, and determined that my

current engagement had run its course for what it could provide to my career path. I needed a change. Faced with the reality that my job had become the most defining aspect of my life, I had a plethora of questions about what I needed from a job to feel fulfilled, and deliberating on those questions led me to ultimately decide that my future was not with my current company.

It was here at this event that I witnessed some of the more painful advice-giving I've ever seen.

This networking event was intimate and formal—the dress code business professional and the venue a small executive boardroom. Twenty of us were seated around an oversized, handsome wooden table, representing all ages and each holding twenty copies of our resumes with an air of nervous excitement. One by one, we stood up, had precisely two minutes to introduce ourselves and our skillsets, pass out our resumes, and explain to the welcoming faces around the table what we were hoping to get out of being present at the event. In their introductions some participants listed off target companies that they were hoping to find contacts at. In other introductions, some people offered up their legal, real estate, or insurance services to local businesses. After the individual finished giving their introduction, the group had an additional two minutes to ask follow-up questions and provide their insight and feedback.

Among everyone getting up and giving their introductions, Jean's situation stood out, and you'll relate to it.

When the spotlight came to Jean, she stood up, introduced herself, and announced that for the last three years post-college she'd held a steady job. However, she was here to ask some important questions to try and get some clarity on whether or not she should leave her industry and explore other careers.

"I have a good job in marketing. I market for a mortgage company. I like the company, I like my work, I like the people I work with. But... to be honest I don't know that I LOVE any of it." And she followed up with: *"I guess I'm here for some guidance, to ask you all—how do you know when it's time to start looking into changing industries or jobs?"*

After a brief silence, and to nobody's surprise, Jean's question was met with something you might've heard more than a few times:

"Just follow your passion!!"

                              "Follow your heart!!"

"Just follow your dreams!!"

                              "Just look inside!!"
            "You already know what you want to do!"

Sitting there as someone in a similar situation, this was fucking excruciating. You know this feeling all too well. When you're in the midst of questioning everything and every life decision you've ever made (ever) and someone offers up a "just follow your passion." Great, thanks. Not particularly helpful.

These statements have a time and a place, but rarely

do they have concrete value in guiding someone to start the long journey that needs to happen before arriving at such a major life decision. That time and place is when someone has already subconsciously made up their mind and just needs a little motivational push. The time and place for dropping enlightening one-liners is not when a lost person is trying to find their way. What if Jean, like everyone, hasn't the slightest clue what "her passion" is? Or what she has to do to "find" it? And whether or not that actually exists or if it's just some hippy-dippy fantasy?

Jean's whole issue here was that she wasn't sure whether mortgage marketing *could* be her passion. And she didn't have the tools to figure it out. I was enthusiastic to hear what guidance our more veteran peers had to offer, but unfortunately I came away feeling less than satisfied. So, I approached Jean after the event to commiserate.

I explained my similar situation and lamented with her that as someone who's in the middle of a career change and going through a lot of soul-searching myself, the absolute *last* thing I need is for another person to tell me to *"Just follow your passion!!"*

Going through one of these question-everything career crises is an emotionally and mentally draining experience, so I expressed my sympathy and decided the best thing I could do for her was to share some of the reflection points that had eventually led me to realize that there wasn't a long-term future for me with my job. This way, instead of staring into the void of the job pool and trying to imagine if *something* out there *could* be better, she could at the very least start by running some reflective studies to identify and define the things that hold weight in these decisions.

I didn't have the answer for how she could follow her passion. But my reflection points were a list of hard-hitting questions that she could use as a launch pad for having an open and honest conversation with herself about where she wants to be.

This book spawned from that conversation, when I realized that the questions I'd built as a personal tool and been asking myself regularly were something that could be valuable to you when faced with the same situation.

Thus, I want to share them with you. Doing whatever I can to help you feel fulfilled, welcome, included, and vulnerable is what *I* find fulfilling, and that's what I hope to inspire with these ideas.

Each coming chapter focuses on an idea to reflect on in your personal journey. We're going to go through aspects of your job, your goals, your feelings, your finances, and your expectations. It's gonna be real. It's gonna be stressful. And it's gonna be fun.

Take a look at these over the years from time to time. They'll give you anchor points to work with.

You already took the first step—opening this book and reading my story. You're doing great. Let's jump right in.

Stop telling me to follow my passion.

Start encouraging me to expand my horizons, try new things, and ask the right questions.

PART I:

Your company, your job, and coping with way too much money

(The part where we get real)

CHAPTER 1:

IF I WON THE LOTTERY, WOULD I QUIT MY JOB?

"When I win the lottery, all my pin boards become reality. Everything will be delicious, covered in glitter, made out of pallets, and look effing amazing."

—*Anonymous Someecards User*

Yep, we're doing it. We're going big. The lottery. Now, the lottery is a fascinating human-made construct that provides us a unique tool for imagination. Obscene wealth beyond anything you've dreamed just minutes away, all based on little numbers on a card you picked up at the gas station on a whim for a couple bucks. The lottery gives us so much wonderful perspective on our otherwise normal lives. You can be a winner, I can be a winner, anybody can be a winner, with absolutely no regard for their socioeconomic status, background, or lifestyle. And because of that, we have no problem imagining ourselves winning that jackpot and walking away with the riches. Man that feels good. So let's see what we can do about harnessing this imagination as a tool for making a vision for improving our lives.

Here's the TL;DR:

- If I won the lottery today, would I quit my job tomorrow?
- Am I trading satisfaction for salary?
- How would I approach having all the free time in the world?

On a crazy hinge while you're filling up your car on your regular commute home, you feel the urge to purchase a Powerball ticket. You can't explain it but everything went perfectly at the office today and it's just feeling like your lucky day. *What the hell, it's just a couple bucks anyway*, you figure. You don't think much about it until you get home and have the TV on while you're cooking dinner.

When it comes time for the drawing your ears perk up. You're absentmindedly watching the numbers on the screen be revealed one by one as you try not to burn your hand because the skillet is still way too damn hot and… wait… that sounded familiar…?

HOLY FUCK

WHAT

HOLY FUCK FUCKING FUCK

NO FUCKING WAY

DUDE I WASN'T PREPARED FOR THIS

I JUST WON $714 MILLION

FUCK

WHAT

LITERALLY WHAT THE FUCK

NOT SURE WHETHER TO DANCE OR THROW UP IN THE SINK

What on earth do you do there? How do you approach this situation? That's not a situation the average person faces. And honestly, if faced with that situation, the average person would seriously fuck it up. Riches easily earned are easily wasted. But regardless, the big question:

Would you quit your job?

Would you immediately march in and give your notice?

Let's explore. If your answer here is no, that you wouldn't quit (or if you're struggling to come up with a concrete answer), this means that there's some inherent value to your personal development as a human that you've assigned to your work. And you've subconsciously determined this value to be beyond money. That's important to pay attention to. When we feel like we're getting something beyond money out of our work situation, that's when we really excel and feel a sense of satisfaction. This is something we

17

should be striving for constantly. I have no doubt you can imagine a slew of jobs that you would love to work if wealth was no question, and equally you can imagine a slew of jobs that you would quit immediately if wealth was taken out of the equation.

I found myself in this boat of knowing that I wouldn't immediately quit my job, but not exactly knowing why. I think it was partially the sense that being in my first job post-college I still had so much to learn just about working life in general, even if it wasn't about specific topics I was passionate about. But I think it was also partially the sense that it was a priority to me as a developing twentysomething to retain a job in order to feel like I was on the right path as a responsible, successful person for my age. Neither of these pointed towards a "passion", but they did point towards value that I assigned to this job.

On the flipside, if your answer to the question was immediately yes, absolutely, you would quit your job—that might be an indicator that in your current situation you're trading your life satisfaction for a salary.

So let's look at that salary. How do you feel about your wages?

Work is a confusing and frustrating crossroads of earning yourself financial freedom and finding something you actually care about doing. It's up to you to determine how much of each you need in order to feel content and satisfied with the balance they give to each other. Say you're feeling unfulfilled at work—if you found a different job opening that was more directly in line with what you want, but it was a 30% pay cut, would you take it? How much weight does your salary have on your job? If you feel like you are in fact trading off fulfillment for a paycheck, think about what kind of pay cut you'd be willing to take if it were a necessary step to advance in the direction of your desired career path.

A friend of mine was faced with a situation like this: he held two competing job offers from different companies in California, one in the bursting tech mecca of the San Francisco Bay Area and one—for lack of a better description—out in the middle of nowhere. Like way out there. The Bay Area offer was for work that interested him more and he liked the city more, but the job out in the middle of nowhere was beating the other offer's annual salary by $25,000. For him this decision got massively complicated because he had many competing factors: location, job function, salary, potential future, etc. Again, these choices are at that crossroads of the countless emotional, logistical, mental, and spiritual factors and are worth some serious, serious reflection. He eventually decided to take the lower-paying offer in the Bay Area on the basis that he was young and wanted to experience city life, and because he identified that job as having greater alignment for his potential futures. As a baseline he knew he would be more satisfied living there and working toward that future.

An interesting fact: there's a study that showed that

after surpassing $75,000 in annual salary, more annual earnings do not correlate to better emotional well-being and mental health[2]. This obviously won't change anything if you're under that line, but if you find yourself making difficult decisions around or above that threshold just know that there is scientific evidence to back up the existence of a roof to how much satisfaction can be brought by bigger bank statements.

Granted, that shit won't be even close to mattering if you pulled in lottery winnings of $714 million. But let's keep working in hypothetical extremes—they're the most telling.

Say winning the lottery means you would quit your job. Why? What are you going to do with your time that's better than that job that you were doing?

This is hinting at the bigger question of what your ultimate desires are. If, for example, your ultimate desire is travel, of course you're going to drop everything and go explore. You have $714 million. You're set.

But that's not for everyone. In the case that your ultimate desire is finding fulfilling ways to apply yourself and your time—this gets more complicated. This isn't something that money can buy. And that's

---

[2] D. Kahneman, A. Deaton, "High Income Improves Evaluation of Life But Not Emotional Well-Being" (2010), Proceedings from the National Academy of Sciences Vol. 107, Iss. 38, http://www.pnas.org/content/107/38/16489.abstract

why you wouldn't quit your job if you were placing an emphasis on the value you were deriving from it prior.

We see this problem all the time in new retirees, they leave their jobs and are faced with the big question of "What now?" Your work is your identity. When faced with the void of that structure not being in place, many people struggle.

When you have all the free time in the world—how are you going to approach that? Where are you going to dive in? Are you going to volunteer? Are you going to go fishing every day up at at the one lake you discovered that's your little secret? Are you going to devote time to family? The church? Organizations you care about? Art projects you've been putting off?

Even personally I'm still working on my answers to these questions because having unlimited free time is something that we can barely wrap our heads around. Digging down to the fundamentals of what you're seeking—fulfilling work, freedom from work at all, travel, philanthropy, or anything else—will help you get more in touch with what you need to do to start walking down those paths. Free time is a concept we'll get back to in coming chapters and explore further. For now, pay attention most to the overarching question. Seriously, what would your gut reaction be if you won the lottery?

CHAPTER 2:

DO I WANT MY BOSS'S JOB?

"By working faithfully eight hours a day, you may eventually get to be a boss and work twelve hours a day."

—*Robert Frost*

Good news. For this one you get to forget about yourself and put your boss under fire. Your supervisor is likely the person most closely tied with your emotional connection to work. They give you assignments, guide your work, and mentor you about the company and its goals and inner workings. In theory, they are your support system and the one demanding the most of you.

TL;DR:
- Do I aspire to fill my boss's shoes?
- Do I prefer functional work over a leadership role?
- Do I have the tools to be successful if I were to take over my boss's job today?

The most important question here—does your boss's job fucking suck? It's entirely possible that your boss is your only line of defense—that without them you would absolutely dread the levels of management above. It's also possible that you feel like they're the lucky one—getting to do the cool, high profile tasks you look forward to doing someday. The role that your boss fills is one we need to get real about. Would you be happy doing what your boss does? Do you aspire to fill their shoes?

In theory, you and your supervisor could be promoted simultaneously up the chain, where your boss would take their boss's job and you would take theirs. If this happened, think about how the new situation would affect your work, your fulfillment, your stress levels, and overall happiness.

You'll need to consider all the factors of their position. Think about the day-to-day tasks that they take ownership of—whether or not you would be happy doing their assignments. Moving up the chain means working with a different set of managers and correspondents. You'll need to be in a good position with these people to be successful in a role traditionally filled by your supervisor. Think about what it's going to take to get to a good standing and set yourself up for success.

For me, I realized that while I admired, liked, and respected my boss, I didn't want his job. Thinking about myself in his position was not something that I looked forward to or aspired to. I took that as a signal that my potential growth opportunities weren't going to be a driving inspirational force for me doing my best work, and that meant that I would *not* be doing my best work. Consequently, this became a point in favor of me leaving my position.

The broader aspect to consider here is whether or not you even want to pursue leadership. It's absolutely okay not to. But let's be clear about what that means.

Society says *you have to be a leader*. But you don't. Not in the classical sense that you need direct reports underneath you. But no matter what you do, you do need to cultivate what we normally think of as leadership qualities. In anything, you need to be courteous, strong-willed, and confident about what you're doing. Take the case of a freelance independent graphic designer—if you want to be your own boss as a freelancer with no supervisors and no underlings, you can make a successful career out of it. But that path doesn't come without the absolute tenacity, drive, and steadfast ambition that we generally attribute to leaders. You need to have the social skills to work with a client base and the business skills to know your worth and stand your ground when clients try and cheat you out of fair value for your effort. Leadership comes in many shapes and forms and it's up to you to decide what it looks like for you.

On the other hand—if you want to be a leader in the classical sense, more power to you. Look at the leaders around you and see what you can learn from them. Not even just business leaders—in local clubs or sports or politics you might find people to look to as inspiration as a leader. Every example you can find will only bolster your vision of what the ideal leader looks and acts like.

Think about whether you want to lead teams or lead yourself. Think about whether you prefer more hands-on functional work like construction or machining or whether you prefer more creative work like designing or coding. Think about if you would be willing to take on direct reports at your current company. If you want to be a classical leader eventually, but don't see yourself doing that at your current company, consider what that means.

The best thing you can do to develop leadership skills and to ensure you're constantly setting the stage for success is to always maintain in your life someone who teaches you and someone whom you can be teaching.

Your teacher might be your spouse, your boss, a coach you hire, your parents, your friends—the possibilities are endless. It could be someone that you never expected. You likely have these people around you already. It's important to have a mentor because you'll look up to them, learn from their leadership style, and determine for yourself what about it is effective or ineffective. I've found role models for myself in family friends, in local organizations, and even at the gym.

And the one you teach could be a junior employee, but this doesn't need to be professional. They could also be a new club member, a child, a younger relative—anyone you can take under your wing. A mentorship is as big or as small of a deal as you make it to be—but know that having a mentee to set an example for will only inspire you in new ways. Teaching someone is what makes *you* an expert in what you're doing and contributes to the future of society. Professionally, I derive a lot of value and reward in taking interns under my supervision and helping them grow their skills. Outside of work, I'm a firm believer in the value of Toastmasters public speaking clubs, and I mentor new members to the organization to help them with their first forays into public speaking.

Look hard to see where these teaching and learning opportunities could be presented through your work. We'll explore your company dynamics more in coming chapters.

To wrap this up, if your answer was yes that you want your boss's job, or even *"hell yeah I'm gunning for her job right now"*, that's an excellent sign. Your ambition is being channeled and you see a future for yourself, at least in terms of position. We have quite a few other aspects of your work that we need to move through and explore, but those kind of reactions would be a positive indicator of you being fulfilled where you are.

And if the question made you doubt whether or not you would actually want your boss's job, that's okay. There are a million reasons why that might be the case and we're going to try and dive more into it in the coming chapters. Know that hesitation here should be met with thinking about the type of career where you *would* absolutely want your boss's job.

CHAPTER 3:

IF I OWNED THIS COMPANY, WOULD I BE PROUD OF THAT?

"Right now, this is a job. If I advance any higher, this would be a career. And if this were my career, I'd have to throw myself in front of a train."

—Jim Halpert, The Office, Season 1, "Health Care"

You're at your current company, everything is the same as any normal day but with one major exception: you're sitting in the CEO's office, behind the desk in the intimidating chair.[3] You're the big boss now. You run the show. No senior execs get their plans through without your approval. You dictate where the company is headed and the timelines for when it will take steps. You have a solid team of leadership underneath you that you trust to <u>run the day-to-day business an</u>d that team leaves you

---

[3] It's true that owning a company and being its CEO are very different functions, but for the sake of this reflection I'm going to be referring to them interchangeably.

to think about the larger strategic picture.

TL;DR:
- Would I be proud of being the CEO of this company?
- Would I sacrifice my work/life balance to lead this company?
- Does owning this company align with my values and long-term goals?

You work long hours, potentially the longest hours. Your employees look to you as a source of inspiration and motivation, and they admire your integrity and tenacity. Your company's Glassdoor rating is determined by *your* ability to keep morale high and employees motivated. Your name is in the news when your company does something big, and you're the one giving high-profile presentations about your company's newest products.

You also take middle-of-the-night emergency calls once every other week. Your significant other puts up with it because they know how much your work means to you. You're in charge, you're the company's champion, and you make convicted decisions at a moment's notice when shit hits the fan. When you own or lead a company, your work and life become intertwined. It's not for the faint of heart.

How does it all feel? Would you be proud of owning your current company?

If you're with a company long enough you can reasonably expect that at one point you'll move your way up the hierarchy into a senior leadership position (possibly even as far as president or CEO). The purpose of this question is to explore these scenarios.

Since our work becomes our identity, we want to work for a cause that we care about. Again, time to dismantle the classical definition of what we mean by "cause". You don't have to work for a nonprofit or a charity in order to find meaningful work for yourself. There are just as many shitty, life-sucking nonprofits out there as there are evil faceless corporations. It's worth mentioning that when we're talking about a cause you care about, a "cause" for some might simply be "making money" and that's completely fair. Companies exist to support their employees in many different ways.

If the cause of your company—your work function, the products you make, the company overall—is something that you believe in, think about how far you'd be willing to take that. Would you be willing to devote weekends and have an offset work/life balance for the sake of your company?

I took a good hard look at whether or not the service that my company offered to the world was something I was genuinely invested in, and ultimately decided it was not. Even though there were good people behind the wheel, I knew that this underlying dissatisfaction around a lack of alignment with my personal ambitions was only going to multiply as I moved up the ladder, and was eventually going to lead me to being very unhappy there.

For you, if your answer is yes (that you would be proud to own your company), congratulations. Your current engagement aligns with your long-term goals and your next steps are going to be around identifying how to get you where you strive to be within your company.

However, if your answer to this is no (that you wouldn't necessarily be proud of owning this company), let's explore what a company you *would* be proud to own might look like. What would a company that aligns with your higher ambitions look like? Dream big, this could be any company that you imagine.

The common reflective prompt for this kind of thing is asking yourself what kind of company you would start if you held a billion dollars in your hands tomorrow. The first step in exploring this billion-dollar question is taking a deeper dive at the contributions to society that you'd like to make through your work. Pretty much any cause you can imagine has a company working to support it, and with the world as connected as it is now, you can find them. Would it be nonprofit? Health care? Technology? Would it be a Tesla? Or a Planned Parenthood? A church? A Mexican restaurant? It's possible that for you, maybe the function doesn't matter as long as you can have happy employees that have enough perks to follow their own dreams.

In the case that you're set and content at your company but there are external causes that you care about deeply, it's worth exploring whether or not your company can find ways to support you as both an employee and a cause-supporter. Some companies offer dedicated volunteer days for employees or match employee donations to charitable organizations. It's a way to encourage social responsibility in the office, shake things up, show care for the individuals of your company, and provide a sense of working towards a higher purpose. If you feel like the causes you care about are supported by your work, bottom line you're going to feel more fulfilled about working there and you're going to be a more productive employee. It's a win-win.

The hypothetical of owning of your company is an intimidating thought—the accountability alone is enough to scare some people from taking up the mantle. The important thing here is being honest with yourself about what you're willing to be responsible for, and whether or not that could or could not be your current company.

CHAPTER 4:

DO I FIND MYSELF VOLUNTARILY TALKING ABOUT WORK, OUTSIDE OF WORK?

"So, what do you do?"

—*Literally everyone*

We all dread it at least a little, but we know it's coming. When you're out with friends and you're introduced to someone new, the inevitable question will come up: "So, what do you do?" Aside from being a safe conversation piece there is undisputable value to asking this question to strangers—potentially finding something in common or a shared interest is a comforting thing to discover about someone. And since work is where we spend the majority of our lives, presumably we have a lot to say about it.

TL;DR:

- Do I feel enthusiastic, annoyed, neutral, or anxious when someone asks me what I do?
- Do I find myself saying things like "It'll pay off in a couple of years..."?
- Am I proud of the work I do here?

Immediately—does the "what do you do" question excite you, annoy you, fill you with anxiety, create a feeling of pride, or not really any of the above?

The things to observe here are the tendencies in your response to this question—a good signal is specifically about how much information you volunteer. There are subtleties to this. Your answer might be short, to get it over with: "Digital marketing." Or your answer might be a little more thorough, inviting the asker to inquire further: "I work for a startup that makes iPhone games that are going to change the world."

You've seen that fire people get in their eyes when they're talking about something that truly gets them fucking stoked. Maybe that's you when you're talking about the latest controversial death in Game of Thrones or maybe it's that one friend when they're getting way too enthusiastic about the fact they trained their cat to crap in the toilet (I mean props to them and the cat), or maybe it's your mom when she's telling you the gossip of your hometown. Enthusiasm is a beautiful thing, to be recognized and encouraged, even if you couldn't care less about your friend's cat. When asked about your work, think about whether or not there's any aspect of it that puts a fire in your eyes when you're talking about it.

Of course, there's certainly the opposite end of the spectrum too. If you find yourself saying things in the realm of: "It's a good position while I wait for the next opportunity" or "it'll pay off in a couple of years", it's worth a good hard think about why that might be the case.

There's a difference between patience and complacence. You can very well be working at goals for yourself that require some serious willpower and acceptance of delayed gratification. Patience and consistent hard work are truly amazing phenomena that humans are capable of, and I have nothing but the utmost respect for people who've found positions they care enough about to buckle down for. But it's important to check in: If what you're working towards or waiting for is a serious couple of years away, consider whether or not you're going to be okay mentally, emotionally, and spiritually with putting in those years. If you're unsure about your resolve with devoting that portion of your life, it might be time to start looking to new paths.

Are you proud of the work you do here? And if you're not, what would work that you would be proud of look like? In that perfect world you fantasize about, what is it you're telling your friends when they ask you about what you do?

When with friends, if you absolutely avoid talking about your work, this might be a warning sign too. Considering how many of our waking hours are spent here, we owe it to ourselves to at least be excited about it occasionally. There's much to be gained with sharing amongst friends, and it's worth observing whether or not you have any interest in voluntarily sharing with your friends about what you have going on at work. Your friends probably have interesting problems they're working through at their jobs too, and they might never share unless you ask them directly. Try it out.

I found that my work provided me occasional blips of something exciting that my equally-nerdy roommates would put up with hearing about. But for the most part it made me discover things that I'm stoked about that were beyond the scope of my job and company—new upcoming projects in the tech industry or fascinating applications of enterprise optimization testing software. And realizing that the things about my work that I was most excited to talk about weren't actually related to my work was a sign for me.

The worst thing you can be doing is faking it. In thinking about our careers we have a tendency to subconsciously look for validation that we're on the right path. And we look for that more with our friends and family than anybody. If you feel like you have to fake excitement about your job to make your friends and family believe you're happy and satisfied, that's a red flag.

Really think about that fire in your eyes and the things that fuel it. The fire comes out when things make you feel alive, whether those are conversations or actions.

Maybe it happens when you solve a problem that you've been banging your head against the wall over for the last four hours. Maybe it happens when you're talking shit with your friends about how much their Fantasy teams suck. Maybe that's when you're doing something adrenaline-producing like getting up in front of a conference to speak. Maybe it's something as simple as having the opportunity to speak with an industry professional that you look up to.

Does your job make you feel alive?

If your answer is yes, try and write down what parts of your job are doing that. That will be significant.

If your answer is no, let's keep asking the questions.

CHAPTER 5:

DO I ADMIRE AND WANT TO BE MORE LIKE THE PEOPLE AROUND ME AT THIS COMPANY?

"People don't leave bad companies. People leave bad managers."
—Enough people that I'm pretty sure this is public domain

The fulfilling nature of work doesn't always come from the actual work itself. Having a good, supportive team that looks out for you and believes in your future is just as important to feeling satisfied at work as the actual job functions that you execute. Where earlier we explored the function of your superior's role, this is going to be an exploration into the actual personalities of the people around you.

TL;DR:
- Do I look up to my peers at work?
- Where in my company can I look for guidance and inspiration?
- Are the people I work with the best or the worst parts of my job?

Just as vital as having admiration for the people around you, your relationship with your supervisor will be paramount to your success. You don't need to be buddies, but there does need to be a mutual respect there. Think about your supervisor and whether or not you feel they have your best interests in mind, they know your goals, and they include you in growth opportunities.

Depending on your company, your relationship with your supervisor may be very formal or very casual, and both are absolutely normal and acceptable. In the most ideal of settings your supervisor is your mentor, but occasionally you'll have to look elsewhere in the company—it's just as important to look at the people around your level and lower in the corporate hierarchy too. It's worth exploring honestly whether you find a sense of safety and support here with those around you. If there's someone who puts a smile on your face just by walking into the office—pay attention to that. Or notice how that one person who kills it in meetings would be your first recruit for an ad hoc project that just came up.

But consider the opposite too, if there's a sense of unhealthy competition or a culture of gossip that's causing you anxiety about your coworkers or supervisor, take that as a red flag. If you're not thrilled about the behavior of the people you work with, step one is to try and do something about fixing it, step two is to ask what implications these kind of things might have on your decision to stay or leave[4].

A healthy relationship with your coworkers looks like this: they lift you up rather then perpetuate workplace politics, they know what you aspire for in your company, and you know what their professional goals are too. You feel like you're improving by being around them and bouncing ideas off them, and you feel comfortable throwing curveball ideas their way because you know they won't judge you.

Having people to look up to is the single biggest catalyst for personal growth. Surrounding yourself with people you admire is the easiest way to guarantee that you'll be pushing yourself and constantly learning. When you spend as much time as we do in the average work day around a group of people, you're bound to pick up on their traits and work ethics. This can go both ways—with the right group you might find yourself more interested and fulfilled than you could imagine. With the wrong crowd you might discover that you only bond over finding things to complain about and dreading work each day, when a different perspective could totally transform these

---

[4] I will never advocate leaving a position without first making an attempt to fix your issues in the workplace. However, if you have a serious workplace issue or feel unsafe at work, you may be better suited to raise the flag to your supervisor or HR department to see if you can align your situation with what you need to feel protected and content.

feelings.

If the people immediately around you aren't people you relate to or revere particularly, where else in your company can you seek guidance and inspiration? Is there another department head whose tenacity you respect? Or another engineer whose creativity you appreciate? Or a manager whose communication leaves you feeling confident in their handling of situations?

At my company I looked up to a variety of different people for a variety of different reasons. I admired one of our executives for his candidness around reducing complexity in major business initiatives. I admired my boss for always having my best interests in mind and for making active efforts to include me in learning experiences. I admired a coworker in another department for the way that she could make everyone laugh, and I admired countless coworkers for their sheer creative talent. This area was a tricky one for me, because while each of these people provided value to the experience I had and to my growth as a new member of the workforce, the satisfaction of our working and personal relationships did not overpower my desire to move into a different industry. This balance is something only you can decide for yourself.

The bottom line is this—if you care about and look up to the people that you work with, your actual job function might be much more fluid in terms of being a determinant of your workplace satisfaction. Some people care only about the specifics of their job function and make it work with any pairing. The best situation is where the two worlds collide—when you like your function and you admire your team.

Are the people you work with the best or the worst parts of your job? Is it that you look forward to getting new assignments or is it that you look forward to the way your boss inspires the team when handing out new assignments?

A supportive, honest, and open culture is one that will create the happiest employees, and as a direct result, the most productive ones too. You owe it to yourself to work in a situation that both challenges and supports you, with people that seek accountability and in turn hold you accountable in a respectful way.

If you find yourself agreeing with the question, that yes, you do admire the people around you, that's excellent news. Pay close attention to *what* you admire about them and take note of what you can learn from them.

If not—if you find yourself surrounded by people that might not be the best supporters of your workplace spirit, try and do something about it first. Talk to HR, voice your discontent, see what *you* can do to improve morale. And if all that is to no avail, start thinking about branching out. You deserve to be around people who inspire you.

CHAPTER 6:

AM I LEARNING OR AM I LEARNING BULLSHIT?

"All the instamodels out there telling me my life is great and to keep kicking ass and I'm just here like man it's more complicated than that."

—Me[5]

Let's rewind to Jean from the Prologue, she was working in marketing for a mortgage company, learning how to market mortgage products. Jean was unsure of whether this skill development was in line with where she wanted to go with her career, but being someone who values hard work and dedication she justified spending her time like this because she was learning a skill.

---

[5] Yes I have the audacity to quote myself, fuck off.

TL;DR:

- Do I feel like I'm learning?
- Is what I'm learning in line with my long term career goals?
- Does my work present me with new opportunities and responsibilities regularly?

At this point you've likely decided that as long as you're learning something at your job you're going to be satisfied with it. But the real question is—is what you're learning a skillset that aligns with your long-term career goals?

The thing to be careful with here is not falling into the trap of feeling like you're learning, when really the things you're improving upon are things you don't give a shit about. If you want to be a designer, learning how to do data entry efficiently is likely not going to be a huge contribution to your craft. Learning how to perfect financial systems is probably not going to make you a better father. Learning the struggle of how to squeeze the most money out of your vendors isn't going to make you a good communicator.

One lie we tell ourselves is that as long as we're learning *something* we're going to be fulfilled by it. But that only gets you so far. Am I learning? Am I learning what I want to be learning or am I justifying "learning" bullshit? Will these things have an impact on my life?

To be clear—there is absolutely value in learning and trying new things, especially new things that you would have never guessed you'd be doing. Sometimes being thrown into new responsibilities can help us realize new facets of our work that we really enjoy or find new hobbies. Being exposed to new opportunities is what keeps us dynamic and growing, and is a vastly important piece of having fulfilling work.

In time, if different work responsibilities that aren't in line with your career aspirations keep building into your schedule, that's going to leave less time for the things you actually care about accomplishing. Getting stuck running customer service telephone lines isn't going to make you a better engineer. It's true that occasionally it'll teach you about how to handle customers and how to interpret their complaints to engineer a better flow to your website, and that's why it can be worthwhile to experience. But if running those phone lines starts taking up 50% of your time, it's up to you to determine if that's a healthy balance and identify what you're getting out of it. If you don't like it, is it worth the dissatisfaction you feel giving up that much time that would be better spent building things?

I had spent a couple years building a division and contributing work that I was genuinely very proud of. But we reached a point where any of my new big learning opportunities were going to be 3-4 years out—once we scaled up and built momentum around our project. In the meantime, I would be handling day-to-day maintenance, which was something that I recognized was not going to make me any more prepared for my long-term career goals. I ran the test:

would I be happy in a holding pattern for three years as we scaled to the point where I could start learning the set of skills that I was excited about? While I would try and justify it to myself by saying that in the meantime I would be learning about maintenance and improving on fundamental project management tools, the answer was clear. That answer was no—I would go fucking bonkers in that holding pattern and needed to switch course into something that would teach me skills I cared about *now*. Because that sense of learning is something that I've identified as carrying heavy weight into whether or not I will feel satisfied at work.

It may seem a little contradictory, but another point I want to stress: give your job a chance. Ask yourself critically if you've been at your engagement for long enough to make it through the honeymoon phase. Every work engagement has a honeymoon and a ramp-up, and only then when things get into their full swing will you start to get a feel for the true colors of your work environment. Don't bail before you get the chance to invest yourself—making this a habit will only cause you to convince yourself that **nowhere** is right for you.

It's up to you to take inventory of your daily tasks to figure out what skills you're developing, and then compare that to your long term plans. You get to choose how much deviation is acceptable and act on that.

PART II:

Your future, your finances, and the worst job you've ever imagined

(The fun part)

CHAPTER 7:

WHAT DO I DO IN MY FREE TIME?

*"I'm too smart to be exhausted **and** bored."*
—Tally Schifrin, Girls, Season 5, "Love Stories"

Hobbies are essential. Hobbies are essential because they help us find balance and explore the things that let us lead a colorful, full life: personal adventures undertaken solely for their enjoyment. A hobby isn't something you do because you have to or because somebody pays you for it. A hobby is something *you* choose for *you.*

TL;DR:
- When I have free time, what do I find myself doing?
- How does this align with my current job?
- Do I feel like my work gives me ample opportunity to explore my own passions?

Maybe you find yourself fascinated with the

intricacies of memes and viral videos. Maybe you're a gamer. Maybe you love to play outside. Maybe you secretly choreograph dance routines that you don't perform for anyone but your pets. Maybe you're passionate about helping animals. You probably have hobbies that you don't even realize are hobbies. Scrolling social media is actually a hobby, yes[6].

What are the things you find yourself doing? Do you find yourself down dark YouTube rabbit holes? What makes you feel centered? Do you create? Do you volunteer? We're not looking at what you *would* do with your free time; we're talking about what you actually observe yourself doing in your free time. What you gravitate toward. These can be very different things, and they might surprise you.

Activities that you gravitate toward are the ones that you don't have to put any effort into convincing yourself to do. We all have activities and hobbies that we *should* do if we just somehow found the free time and the willpower. But it's not much of a hobby if you have to drag yourself to doing it.

I realized there was a huge discrepancy between what I thought of as my hobbies and what I actually gravitate toward. If you'd asked me what I like to do, or if you're a dating app that prompts me to try and come up with ways to make myself enticing to the preferred sex, I would start with "hiking." You probably would too, let's be real. But I never go hiking. I just don't.

---

[6] Albeit a destructive one, some would argue.

It's not something I gravitate toward. Same with going to concerts or cooking. I do genuinely enjoy all those things, but I don't do them without deliberately making conscious effort or feeling like I *should* because society says this will make me a normal, date-worthy individual.

I gravitate toward video games and sending pictures of cute dogs to my favorite people. I gravitate toward reading summarized versions of tech discoveries online. I gravitate toward FaceTiming people even when I know they're busy. I gravitate toward trying to get together a group of friends to go to a park and play wiffleball. These are things I do without putting any effort into them. What do you gravitate toward?

Then the further question becomes this: is there alignment between what you gravitate toward in your free time and your employment? And if there isn't, what can you do to make it so there is?

One clue to pay attention to is whether you feel energized or stifled after a day at work. When you come home and want to conquer the world, that means you draw inspiration from your work situation. And even though "conquering the world" might look like cooking dinner and reading a good book, it's in the outlook. When you come home and want to crumple on the couch, it's an indication that you may be unhappy.

Not to say you won't have hard or draining days at work. That's just part of the natural cycle. But you don't deserve to be in a relationship with your work that leaves you feeling down every day. And if you truly don't have free time due to your work situation, you will not be able to maintain a healthy life balance. This is an unsustainable scenario.

In thinking about your present moment in the context of the future, a certain late Apple CEO put it well.

"For the past 33 years I have looked in the mirror every morning and asked myself: "If today were the last day of my life, would I want to do what I am about to do today?" And whenever the answer has been "No" for too many days in a row, I know I need to change something."

—*Steve Jobs*

Even though this quote is phrased morbidly, thinking about *today* and your feelings about *today* is a digestible, strategic step to take in determining the mentality to take into tomorrow. You have control of your life and your situation. The universe is here to support you in helping you find and follow your dreams.

There's another key factor—one that might come up in the case where you're content with your work setup and the lifestyle it allows you to lead. If your work isn't necessarily something you're passionate about, do you feel like your work situation gives you ample opportunity to explore your own passions?

You might have started this chapter going "lol, free time? What's that?" A relevant example was a friend who was working two part-time jobs and it was giving him an unpredictable, 7-days-a-week work schedule. He decided that having regular free time mattered more to him so he traded those part-time gigs in for a single full-time job and while the work wasn't absolutely in line with where he wanted to go, the activities he could pursue in the regular free time it offered mattered more to him, and that was where he would find his fulfillment. Different strokes for different folks.

Similarly—say you've even identified that you're passionate about a vocation that unfortunately, under normal circumstances, doesn't produce a livable income, like oil painting. You love oil painting more than anything and constantly yearn to find ways to paint more, and maybe eventually even get paid for it. But unless you're in the top percentile of a percentile of painters, you're going to realistically still need a day job to support yourself. For you, the question then becomes whether or not the work situation you've built for yourself is one that can support you in your oil-painting pursuits.

Your hobbies are an incredibly telling part of your identity, and being in tune with them will be vital to understanding what motivates you. The exciting thing about them is that because you design them for you, you get to experiment with them as much and as often you'd like.

CHAPTER 8A:

MY THREE 5-YEAR PLANS

"So, where do you see yourself in five years?"
—That unenthusiastic interviewer who rescheduled you twice

You've probably faced the five-year question a few times. And you probably think about it occasionally in two situations: when pulling at strings on a bad date, and when preparing for job interviews. Well, the good news is that it *can* actually be a pretty useful reflection tool, when presented with a twist. Prepare to have your world rocked.

The idea this chapter is built around is credited to Stanford Professor Dave Evans, former Apple engineer and co-founder of Electronic Arts (with credentials like those, damn.) Professor Evans brings us a unique concept that he calls Odyssey Planning and it's worth your time. It'll be the most significant step you'll take to realizing that you are the master of your own destiny. Paralleled only by a good reading of *The Alchemist* maybe.

TL;DR:

- An experiment: create three separate, totally different five-year plans for myself.

The problem Professor Evans aims to address is that, as humans we have a tendency to frame our life outlook in terms of finding our *one true* passion: "How do I figure out that one perfect solution to my life? How can I be sure that I'm doing the right things to maximize my life and my happiness?"

To rebuff this and uncover an answer, Professor Evans has a unique project for his students. The day-one assignment is this: come back to class next week with three completely different five-year plans for yourself.

As the reader, your task is to think about this, even for a few seconds. If it resonates, dive into it. I took a personal day to isolate myself away from the hustle and bustle and find a quiet café where I could sit alone with my thoughts. I brought a journal and wrote about this, and that was one of the biggest turning points for me[7].

This exercise is significant because chances are you're planning to be happy in five years. Chances are you're not going to be designing a future for yourself where

---

[7] I was originally going to leave some blank pages here for you to fill out, but I realized that authors have been attempting to do that for years and nobody ever actually uses them. Great in theory, terrible UX in practice.

you're fucking miserable. That means your five-year plans will all end with you being happy, and when diving into this idea what that knowledge, you're going to understand that there isn't *one true destiny* for you. There are many things you could be doing that you would find fulfilling.

*"The question 'is this **really** your passion?' sets an unrealistically high bar that you will never reach."*
—Dave Evans, The Hidden Brain Ep. 56, Getting Unstuck

For me in my situation, I came up with three grand plans. One where I left California immediately and went to graduate school for Data Science in Austin, TX and then moved into a career in that field. I made another plan where I took an unpaid internship for a couple of months to learn new skills and widen my job prospects while I rounded out my lease in Orange County. And lastly, I had a plan where I did neither of those things and moved up to San Francisco to start a people operations consulting business. Extensively playing out each of these situations was astonishing for me because it felt like my world opened up in that exploration—and I built a vision for the kind of person I want to be in a broader sense.

Pretty weird though, isn't it? The purpose of this exercise is to illustrate to you that you can create your future. Life will throw you a lot of curveballs that'll knock you from your idea of your ideal path. And that's okay. You'll be fine. These curveballs will just work themselves into the path that you're actually manifesting and you'll be the better for it.

The next step in the exercise is to figure out how to dip your feet into each of these potential five-year paths, what Professor Evans calls "prototyping". If that means taking an introduction class online or speaking to a friend who does something more in line with those paths, the first steps can be small and simple. I found courses I wanted to take online, free community workshops that I could attend, mentors to speak with about consulting, and informational sessions regarding graduate school. These were simple first steps that made me feel like there were real, tangible trails I could follow.

Personally, discovering Professor Evans' Odyssey Planning concept was one of the most absolutely comforting moments in my journey, and now I find myself all the time thinking back to that personal day I took to sit, write, and imagine these futures. In the process of identifying which paths you're interested in pursuing and what your life could look like, this is the most effective way to start.

CHAPTER 8B:

DETAILING A FUTURE DAY

"Now dream small. Dream the little dreams that fit life now, but point those little dreams at the big dream. Small dreams and big dreams require the same to find fulfillment."
—Todd Smith, Enliven Wellness Coaching

Future-thinking is what keeps us going. Your thoughts about your career aspirations are what led you to pick this book up in the first place. In complement to Professor Evans' three-five-year-plans assignment, I have another quick exercise for you.

Post-graduation, a friend of mine was looking for guidance and decided to invest in herself by hiring a career coach. I was struck by and admire the conviction and vulnerability that took, and as someone who aspires to be a mentor in the future, I was thrilled to hear about the exercises they would go through together. Of all of their lessons together, one in particular resonated with me most and became a regular reflection point in own life.

TL;DR:
- Five years down the road, what does an ideal day look like for me—by the minute?
- What does my morning routine look like?
- What's different between this vision and what I'm currently doing?

In addition to the five years plans we just went through, we're going to go through another take on your future-planning. Here's the kicker: instead of the broad, sweeping picture, we're getting down to the specifics. Try this: take one of your five-year plans and walk through a day-in-the-life, in painstaking minute-by-minute detail. Explore every single little piece of it:

In the morning: What time are you waking up? How big is the bed you're getting out of? Or was it a hammock? Do you get dressed immediately? Do you workout? If so, where? What kind of exercise? How long? Do you shower? What do you eat for breakfast? What else is part of your morning routine? How much time do you build in to yourself before heading off to work? Where are you? How long is your commute? How do you commute? Do you commute?

In the office, think about what your routine will be. What is the first thing you do when you get into the office? Do you work in an office at all? What does your team at work look like? What do you hope to accomplish in the morning before lunch? Do you bring your lunch or go out to lunch? Do you take your lunch by yourself and enjoy your peace and quiet or do you recharge instead by spending time eating with your coworkers?

At the end of the workday but before you leave, do you have a concluding routine to prepare for the next day?

What do you do on your commute home? Do you call family? Do you listen to podcasts or music or audiobooks or silence?

In five years, do you meet up with friends after work? For a drink or for dinner or to discuss potential business ideas? Do you go to play sports? Or donate your time to the community?

And so on. What do you do once you're back at your home? Do you have any pets? Do you have roommates? What is your relationship to them? What does your home look like? How is it decorated? How does it feel to enter that space? How does it smell? Do you live alone? Do you have a partner? What does your evening routine look like? What do you wear to bed? What time do you go to bed?

Think about every detail. You get to create this future. Use your imagination. Make it fun. Make it silly.

The key question to note here: what's different between this five-year vision and what you're doing right now? Chances are you're going to find out that very little is holding you back from implementing some of this vision into your life right now.

By diving into the details we're able to build a fuller, more complete vision for our definition of success. And it helps us determine the pieces of our day that we assign weight to in calculating what makes a good day. This is different for everyone, and as an exploration is a worthwhile, amusing adventure to take towards personal wellness.

CHAPTER 9:

WHAT WILL I NOT DO?

"Where should we go for dinner?"
—Guaranteed relationship drama

Just as important as it is to explore the ideas of what you *want* to do, it's equally valuable to think about the worst shit you can possibly imagine doing for work. Honing in on what you're truly interested in is a frustratingly abstract task and any fresh angle you can take will be a good use of time and brainpower.

TL;DR:
- What am I *not* willing to do?
- Do I like facing clients?
- Would I scoop shit?

First, a familiar situation. How many times have you been faced with this—you're sitting there with your friend or your significant other debating what you should do for dinner and going round and round in a circle of:

"What do you want?"
"idk whatever you want."
"idk whatever you want sounds good."

Not very helpful, right? One of the most effective lessons we can learn about approaching these situation is looking at them from the side of negative synthesis.

*"Okay well what do you **not** want?"*
"Hmmmm well I'm getting sushi tomorrow so not fish."
"Okay what about pizza?"
"No I've had that for the last three meals straight and while that's not a problem I do feel like I should balance that out with an assorted selection of organic leafy green things."
"Chipotle it is."

See how much more effective that conversation is?

As humans, we're way better at identifying things we *don't* like than we are at imagining or identifying things that we do like, or that bring us joy. Armed with that knowledge, how can we turn that into something useful?

In career exploration, we can apply this to your work. Instead of facing into the void of "okay, what do you ideally want to do for work?", we can turn this on its head. What do you *absolutely not* want to do for work? Where is your threshold for work you won't put up with?

Would you not scoop literal human shit? Would you not make your living by being an exotic dancer? Obviously those are extremes, but both are perfectly viable sources of income with countless wonderful people working them.

To have a manageable jumping-off point, we start with simple questions and break it down. Try asking yourself questions like these:

- Will you only work in sales?
- How do you feel about manual labor?
- Do you need an element of creativity? If so, does it need to be artistic?
- Can you survive the way you want on minimum wage?
- Do you need absolute guidance and structure?
- Do you want to be client-facing? Or would you rather do the backend work without ever facing the client?
- Do you need numbers and problems with clear, absolute answers?
- Will you absolutely not travel for work? Will you only accept jobs that make you travel for work?
- Are there jobs that you dream about that you need special training for? What would it take to get that training?

And so on. Make a list. Get brutally honest. What will you not put up with? Identify your floors for these kind of things.

My first step was identifying some aspects that I would absolutely not be happy doing: corporate finance, repetitive data entry, working for a company whose products I don't use or get excited about, anything in a typical sales capacity, and anything that would require me regularly working holidays or weekends. These gave me a bottom line to work from.

From there I was able to get a little more specific about what I wanted and needed:

- Working around engineers
- Working in a household-name tech company
- Living in a major city in the US
- Ideally more internal-facing than client-facing
- Paying above minimum wage
- In a capacity that would require daily human interaction

This established a solid basis, but left the door open to many different careers offered by these companies like data science, HR, product management, recruiting, etc. Any of these capacities could fit my new criteria, and identifying these criteria gave me the launching points needed to effectively start my job search.

One thing that might surprise you (it certainly surprised me) is that you have a natural aversion to any job that you consider "hard work", whether or not you're aware of it. But this is an interesting contradiction to the human condition.

Again as humans, we naturally actually really like hard

work. We may not feel that we like it because it's, well, *hard*, but this difficulty turns out to be exactly why we enjoy it. We're hard-wired to problem solve and to feel awesome doing it. This is why we get bored doing the same thing for long enough and why we're stimulated by new challenges. There's an endless sea of people out there who will complain about their work (because complaining about work is what we do as a society), when secretly they love their work. That secret might even be a secret from themselves. Noticing our natural aversion to what we subconsciously view as "hard work" means that we get to choose to ignore that aversion and plunge into something different, exciting, and new. A new challenge, a new set of "hard" problems, or a new environment might be what you need in order to be invigorated in doing your best work, and that task that we think of as "hard" might be just what we need.

When approaching the big scary questions like "what do I want to do with my life", it's imperative that we take advantage of every tool available, and sometimes imagining the absolute worst can be a surprisingly valuable, insightful, and (somewhat) entertaining way to start.

BONUS CHAPTER:

IS IT POSSIBLE TO MOVE INTERNALLY TO A BETTER-SUITED POSITION FOR ME?

"Another one."

—*Khaled Mohamed Khaled*

Chances are if you work for a big enough company, there's an established system for moving around between departments or groups within the company. It's to their benefit to retain high-performing employees, even if it means reassigning them. They'd rather see you happy in a different role than see you leave altogether. Turnover is *expensive*, ramping up new employees is *expensive*, and fitting new employees into your culture and workflow culture takes a long time and resultantly is—you guessed it—*expensive*.

Therefore, they want to keep you. The question then becomes whether or not you want to keep them.

If your company offers these reassignment services,

you should absolutely be looking into them at first doubt of your job satisfaction. These are rare opportunities that people at smaller companies don't get and they offer you the safety net of exploring other career paths, locations, and growth opportunities while keeping a friendly reputation with both sides of the equation. You'll be supporting the same company regardless, and you're going to be doing your best work in a position that you're being most satisfied with. Therefore, it's in everybody's best interests to try and get you into a role that's bringing out your best. Consider as an exercise taking the time to write out your ideal job description and then start by taking a look at whether or not any internal listings align more with this ideal than what you're currently doing.

While moving internally is not a sure thing, it's always worth exploring as a first response. Being able to explore other opportunities with the confidence that your company will have your back and maintain your benefits is a huge relief in the soul-searching process.

Get coffee with someone from every department that you're even mildly interested in. You never know where it'll take you—and it doesn't hurt to get to know a little bit more about them.

Don't shut any doors before they're even open.

CHAPTER 10:

HOW LONG CAN I SURVIVE WITH MY CURRENT FINANCIAL STANDING?

"Money isn't the most important thing in life but it's reasonably close to oxygen on the 'gotta have it' scale."

—*Zig Ziglar*

The point of this book is not to help you justify making a reckless decision. While leaving a job can feel dangerous, when it's thoughtfully planned for, the stress and strain can be minimized. All of these reflection points are for when you're feeling lost specifically in your **career** and have the reasonable means to take a risk and explore alternative paths should you choose to do so. Obviously there are countless external responsibilities (family, debt, medical bills, etc.), priorities, and sources of fulfillment outside of your work that factor into any of these decisions and that should be heeded with the appropriate weight. With any of this, be smart, calculated, and convicted. With that, let's explore the considerations that you need to be aware of before making a big decision.

Let's say hypothetically you've created a vision for yourself that involves quitting. Let's run with that vision and make sure that it's fully formed before it comes to any manifestation. It's time to make budgets. Not having an income stream is maybe one of the most fundamentally fucking stressful things a human can go through. Suddenly every decision you make has significantly more weight. Do you get that dinner with friends? Or do you need that cash for your car payment?

TL;DR:
- Do I have the financial backing to support myself in unemployment for six months?
- What other financial obligations are looming over my decisions?
- Are there any vesting or profit-sharing plans I need to be considering with my employer?

The bottom line: make sure you've been saving enough to give yourself a few months of wiggle room. The general rule of thumb is to keep enough cash on hand to support yourself for six months in case shit hits the fan and you lost your job today.

Remember, when you're unemployed you have zero paid-for benefits. If you're under the age of 26 (as current legislation stands), you're still eligible to be a dependent on your parents' medical, dental, and vision coverages, which can get you better deals on those coverages. But if you're on your own, you need to factor in these costs. Medical is *expensive*. Depending on your age and any dependents we're talking potentially thousands of dollars a month.

Also consider any outstanding debts you might have. Mortgages, car payments, and student loans are all heavy weights. You'll need to be prepared to cover these while in your transition. What financial obligations are you facing within these decisions?

In all likelihood your lifestyle is going to radically change once you're unemployed.

In addition to straight budgeting, there are other considerations to make that your employer might be using to incentivize keeping you. If you're getting a 401(k) match or stock options, are there vesting schedules you need to be paying attention to? Since these can be considered "free money", they can make a significant impact on your retirement plan and shouldn't be taken lightly. Will three more months vest your employer contributions or stock options? Then it might be worth sticking around for that.

Finding a job can take a long time. However long you're thinking it'll take you—plan for twice as long. I did the recommended six-months'-expenses savings plan along with some additional so I could take time off and travel between working and job-hunting. I thought it would take me three to four months max to lock down a job. I made it to six months of unemployment before I could pick up some part-time consulting work to pay the bills while I continued my search for full-time employment. I ended up moving into my childhood room back home with my mother in order to not pay rent. And that was okay—as I took the leap I knew these would be realistic scenarios and I had planned for them.

If you're going to put yourself in the flux of unemployment, your plan is going to be what's going to get you through. Obviously the simplest method is to line something up *prior* to quitting, but sometimes life doesn't work that smoothly. If you have a clear idea of industries or projects you want to explore, it can be the smoothest move to quietly spread your feelers out while still employed and start your journey without having to navigate the uncertainty of unemployment. There's certainly a peace of mind to be gained for lining up your next gig, but if you need to take time to yourself between jobs to reflect or work on personal projects or travel, this may not be totally possible.

Another option to consider: if you decide you need to get out *now*, are there any opportunities for short-term transitional work to support yourself with while giving you the time to develop the skills you need or to look for your next opportunity? This might look like part-time freelance work, helping in the community, driving for a rideshare, contributing content-writing to that friend who runs their own small business, or even doing odd jobs.

To be clear, this isn't to advocate that you stick with a job that you're unhappy with solely because you financially *have* to, the point here is to make you aware of the many considerations you're going to realistically face that can be intimidating when you switch off your income stream.

PART III:

Putting it all together, and how to quit
without looking like an asshole

(The next steps.)

CHAPTER 11:

WHAT TO EXPECT

"NO REGRETS."
—Somebody with an unrealistic grasp on how making a major life decision plays out

Unfortunately, there's no scoring system for whether or not you should leave your job. There's no "add up your answers and here's where you fall on the spectrum." As mentioned before, employment is a unique combination of emotional, mental, financial, spiritual, and personal factors that all play a part of making these decisions (and unfortunately making them really goddamn complicated.)

These questions have been what you *can* look at. If you're not loving your situation, reflecting on them will be a major tool in processing the complicated emotions and logistics of changing careers. Hopefully they've either helped you feel more secure and fulfilled with what you're doing right now, or they've helped you make the realization that it might be time to start thinking about moving on.

Either way, be honest. Be vulnerable. Nobody is going to harass you for the answers. This is solely a tool for you.

At this point you're probably either feeling lost, inspired, or like reading this book was a colossal waste of time. No matter which of those describes your situation, I appreciate you bearing with it. If I could buy you tacos right now I would.

This chapter is for those of you who have decided that your career needs a second look. If you're here thinking that it's time to quit—here's what you can expect in the coming situations:

(1) It's gonna be overwhelming

When you take the first step away from something that's tying you up mentally and emotionally you're going to be hit with strange and overwhelming waves of freedom and anxiety. I had an equal number of days where I woke up feeling crushed by lack of direction and equal days where I woke up like "Hell yeah I'm the motherfucking champion of my life and everything I do today is going to be because I *decide* to."

The shock that accompanies leaving a job is the kind of trial we don't get to go through many times in our life. It's a little terrifying. But it can be harnessed to learn about yourself and make your true colors show. Putting yourself in a place where you can have mental freedom is only the first step along the road to revealing your passions. These uncomfortable, challenging, unnerving states of transition are where we find out what makes us tick.

But first and foremost: take a second to enjoy the freedom of the weight lifted off your shoulders.

Be proud of yourself for taking a step outside of your comfort zone and taking charge of your life.

Be proud of yourself for having conviction.

(2) Regret is normal

I had nightmares about leaving my job for the couple of weeks *after* leaving my job because my subconscious decided that removing that structure from my life meant that my world was crumbling around me and it needed to remind me of that.

Regret is a frustratingly human trait. You're going to have some amount of regret for leaving a comfortable situation no matter what. This doubt is a survival mechanism. You stepped away from your comfortable situation that was helping you survive, how dare you? Your body and mind are naturally going to rebel, and make you feel bad for tearing them away from their comforts.

You will feel regret because of societal pressures. It sucks, but it's inevitable. What will my friends think of me quitting? What will my parents think about my "reckless" decision? The fear of regarding yourself as someone who "gave up" is a tough one. But truth is, nobody will think of you like that. They'll be seeing you as someone who moved on to bigger things.

Deciding to be alive is reckless. It's scary. It's exciting. It's what gives us our humanity. Those are feelings to relish. The freedom you feel is a unique thing—embrace it. There's absolutely nothing wrong with experiencing regret—it's when we refuse to acknowledge our feelings that they consume us. Take note of these emotions and know that you'll be okay.

If you're starting to think that your job is not serving your needs, it's time to explore why you haven't taken action: what you're worried about and what you're afraid of. What are the fears and pressures that have led you to stay where you are? Are you just comfortable, or are you alive? Once we identify this, we can act on it.

The biggest fear we have as humans is the fear of living—of pursuing the things that light our soul on fire. We are raised into a society that presents us with an idea of what success looks like and pressure to conform to that comfortable standard. But we as humans have the power to become aware of that pressure and decide against it—to decide to live on our terms. Terms that might not always be the most comfortable. But terms that we craft out of intention.

If it's the right thing for your future and your development, quitting does **not** mean you're giving up. It means you're putting yourself first. And you'll prosper and grow from taking that risk.

I'll get off my soapbox now, but make sure that you're doing this because it's the best thing for you.

(3) Enjoy your free time, but make sure to DO

In my transition I crossed a couple things off my bucket list, and that felt like a genuine, human accomplishment. And then I started furiously networking, taking online classes, and attending community events around the kind of technologies and companies I wanted to get involved with. I learned everything I could about emerging tech projects, met hordes of helpful acquaintances, and developed skills through courses while doing it. And I made sure to take advantage of having precious weekday free time to play outside as much as possible.

Give yourself time to adjust. Don't rush into your next job, even if you have one lined up back-to-back. Take a vacation for yourself and get back in touch with the things and hobbies and activities that make you smile stupidly. Are there friends who bring out your ridiculous side that you've been neglecting? Are there lawn games that you've put aside because you've been too busy? Is there a trip you've been dreaming about but have been putting off until you had enough vacation time? Take advantage of this time to get back in touch with what living means to you. This is a realization that can only come from you—and is paramount to you figuring out your next steps.

Time away from working is such a rarity—when the majority of Americans get 2-4 weeks of paid time off a year, getting an additional little chunk of time in transition is something to be cherished.

The important thing is to not let yourself stagnate. Make sure to be DOING. Staying productive with your time off will be the number one thing that'll keep your mood and attitude up and keep you afloat. Structure your time to support the steps you're taking to progress into your next career. Take classes. If you're into artistic pursuits, try that one you've been putting off. If you think you might be into coding, take online courses and get a foundation. Now will be the time when you have the most creative freedom you've ever had. Take advantage of it in your journey. If you spend this time sitting around waiting to "discover yourself", sooner or later you're going to realize nobody ever took a step to uncovering a passion by doing nothing. This is something that only comes through action.

In that path of "finding your passion", the best thing you can do is try everything. See if you can get informational interviews with people in the industries you're curious about. Sit down with that nurse for coffee. Don't be afraid to reach out. Everyone is willing to spend 15 minutes with someone in the interests of helping them get a better grasp on the world. What research can you do to best prepare yourself to interview or succeed in your next job?

You can expect to start living on a tighter budget now that you don't have income. You can expect to start cooking more than you eat out. You can expect to have more free time than you've expected. You can expect to get bored. Again, these are things to be embraced and used as tools for figuring out what matters to you.

Know this: it'll be okay. Nine-to-fives aren't going anywhere, and you'll be able to work for the rest of your life if you want to. It's harder to spend your time playing and enjoying precious moments—so take advantage of the opportunity you just made for yourself.

Life is too short to waste our time doing things we don't feel are contributing to our greater growth.

You've worked hard. You've proved yourself. You're doing great.

You'll be just fine.

If at this point you're considering taking the plunge, the next chapter is focused on the actual etiquette of quitting, all the practical steps and considerations that need to be taken to leave on a good foot.

CHAPTER 12:

THE ETIQUETTE OF QUITTING

"There's a trick to the Graceful Exit. It begins with the vision to recognize when a job, a life stage, a relationship is over—and to let go. It means leaving what's over without denying its value."
—*Ellen Goodman*

If you do go ahead and decide that it's time to look into other careers, you'll eventually need to give notice of your resignation. The personal nature of this situation can be anxiety-inducing because of the relationships that are involved. Since giving notice can be a bit murky and a bit awkward, I've broken it down into a couple different areas to focus on in preparation.

Transition plan:
Before you give notice, take thorough inventory and list out everything you do at the company. You want to be courteous to your employer and sensitive about making the transition as smooth as possible. Will your role need to be filled? What tasks are specific to you

that you'll need to train others on? Start putting together a plan on how you'll transfer your duties over to other team members.

Timing:
A big question that comes up all the time: how much notice is appropriate to give? Conventional professional courtesy is generally two weeks. While two weeks is not required by law, your company policy might state that certain notice must be given to avoid forfeiting accrued vacation day payouts or other benefits. Check your employee handbook for your specific company policy. Gauge the situation and figure out how long it would take the company to replace you. If you're a higher-level manager, it might call for more notice because you'll have a harder spot to fill.

However—*it's equally important to not give notice too far in advance.* The moment that you give notice of your resignation, everything changes. As soon as it's been established that you'll be leaving, you'll find yourself being treated differently. And you'll find yourself subconsciously checking out, not being ultimately productive or doing your best work. That's just natural. To leave on the best foot, find the middle ground between just enough and not too much.

Notice Letter:
Put your notice of resignation in writing, something with your signature on it. It's absolutely necessary to include the following:
- Today's date (date of notice)
- Statement of resignation

- What your last day will be

Keep it short and sweet.

Here's what mine looked like. Feel free to steal it.

<Today's Date>

Dear <Supervisor>,

After much consideration, I have made the difficult decision to leave the <Company> team to pursue other endeavors. I am incredibly grateful for my time at <Company> and sincerely appreciate the skills and growth I've been able to realize through my time here. I wish you and the company all the best moving forward.

Effective today I am giving my notice of resignation, and my last day with <Company> will be <Date>. I will be providing a transition plan to make sure everything goes as smoothly as possible.

Sincerely,
<Your signature>

Try to deliver your notice in person. It's scary, but it's respectful and sincere.

Keep your contacts:
If there are any people you've met through the company that you've particularly enjoyed working alongside and would like to stay in touch with, email them individually to thank them for your great working relationship and pass along your personal

contact information. Are there external account managers that have handled your company gracefully and professionally? Are there clients that you vibe with? You'll never be able to estimate the power of networking until it comes in handy down the road.

Don't burn any bridges:
Meet 1-1 with the major stakeholders in your employment at the company to explain your situation. The more you communicate, the more sympathy and support you'll receive. You never know where your career is going to take you and whether or not you'll be working with these people again, so always, always, leave on a good foot. The better your relationships are, the more understanding your coworkers will be of a decision to leave to go better yourself. The only situation where leaving doesn't go over well is when you've already checked out and aren't performing or participating. Generally, people are pretty receptive to one's pursuits in self-growth. Write cards or emails to your favorite people at the company, and stay in touch. You never know when they'll pop up later in your career. And freaking connect on LinkedIn. I've had countless contacts from my professional past circle around years down the line, and I've ended up working with some of my favorites at multiple companies.

All in all, being graceful in how you handle your exit from a job can have constructive long-term impacts. Even though you might fantasize about going out Office Space-style, burning the building down (figuratively or not), I'm really going to advocate being courteous and straightforward.

But hey, I'm not the boss of you.

WRAPPING IT UP

"I need a drink."

—*You, probably*

And that's it, we're done. Nice work. Deep breath. Pat on the back.

We just spent time exploring different aspects of your current engagement, your ideas about what defines success in your future, and all the real-world considerations you need to be taking when thinking about any of this.

This book was a challenge, and it achieved its goal if it sparked any honest conversation within yourself on whether or not you're satisfied with what you're doing at this moment in time.

I went through this process and it was terrifying. Terrifying, but very cathartic. Being honest and vulnerable with myself about what I need and what I demand was a life-changing experience. I planned meticulously and saved enough money to give myself a couple months of exploratory time. My family called it "calculated recklessness." I give you all this insight from my first person. And I share it because I believe in helping others find what makes them happy, what makes them feel alive.

Additionally, I want to point out it's likely that in diving into these questions you exposed one or two specific things about your company that you're unsatisfied about. It's not enough to throw your hands up in the air and quit as a response. Your responsibility first is to acknowledge those things and try and do something about them. No company is perfect, and you have the power to be the catalyst for changes you want to see in the office.

If you found this helpful, I want to hear about it. If you thought it was horseshit, I want to hear about it. If it changed something about your life, I want to hear about it. If you thought it was just a good read but you're solid where you are, I'd love to hear that too. I want to hear from you about your journey. If you're comfortable with it, it would mean the world if you could leave your story with the community at www.wickwrites.us/forum. I'm only one perspective, and everyone will grow hearing about the decision process you went through too.

And if you know someone who needs this book, pass it on. If you need it as a reminder, keep it.

It'll be okay. It'll all be okay. The universe will work out in exactly the way it's meant to.

Thanks for listening. These things are tough and "just following your passion" isn't the most helpful piece of advice we can hear. Here's to wishing you all the best in your journey. Go get some tacos.

Cheers,
Wick

ACKNOWLEDGMENTS/WONDERFUL HUMANS I OWE THIS TO

- I am grateful to my mother for the inspiration and the HR-related coaching, and for being not only my mother but my best friend, temporary landlord, and cheerleader through the processes that shaped this book.

- I am grateful to Jean for having the courage to ask for guidance to our roundtable group and kicking off the idea for this creation.

- I am grateful to Grayson Roze for paving the way, opening me to the idea that I can be an author, and for being not only the realest of friends but a personal and business teacher as well.

- I am grateful to this book's MVP and my coach extraordinaire Sarah Eisenberg for helping me craft my existential crisis into coherent thoughts, for teaching me how to organize my rants into constructive ideas, for teaching me to tastefully swear, for the all-hours FaceTime sessions when I was feeling stuck, and for her extensive time reading and reviewing all my drafts. Hands down, she put an exceptional amount of time into this book and into my development as a writer, and I can safely say this wouldn't have happened without her.

- I am grateful to Jodi Naglie for having the conviction to invest in herself and hire a coach, and for being willing to share with me the invaluable and profound lessons she picked up in that adventure. It meant the world to me to be included in that journey.

- I am grateful for my editors:

  o Reed Halberg, especially for his technical specificity. Who the fuck knew the English language has three different types of dashes that all have different grammatical uses? Reed did.

  o Will Kellogg, especially for his holistic and wholesome perspective. Somehow we're always on the same page but able to come at things from completely different angles.

  o David Corley, especially for his grammatical genius. He gave me the peace of mind needed to finally say "this is done."

- I am grateful to Dave Evans for his Odyssey Planning ideas and my brother for introducing me to the podcast where I learned the concepts. They've changed my life for the better.
- I am grateful to my sister for keeping my sanity in check with gifs, board games, and thoughtfulness.
- I am grateful to Chapman University for the most formative years of my life, for my education, for my growth, and for their amazing alumni events. These roundtables are incredibly cool and I think attendees derive a lot of value from them. The intimate, formal, facilitated structure can't be beat. Sorry I had to use one as a bad example <3
- I am grateful to the companies and supervisors that I've been lucky enough to work for, and for their understanding and support of my situation and decisions.

REFERENCES

- NPR's The Hidden Brain Episode 56: Getting Unstuck ft. Dave Evans
- Girls, Season 5, Episode 9, "Love Stories"
- The Office, Season 1, Episode 3, "Health Care"
- D. Kahneman, A. Deaton, "High Income Improves Evaluation of Life But Not Emotional Well-Being" (2010), Proceedings from the National Academy of Sciences Vol. 107, Iss. 38, http://www.pnas.org/content/107/38/16489.abstract

ABOUT THE AUTHOR

Wick is an Austin, TX-based[8], nervous, thought-filled wreck who's quit his fair share of jobs. He's that friend who asks the annoyingly probing questions about the things you're thankful for and the things you're looking forward to when you were just trying to shoot the shit, jeez man.

Professionally, he also writes occasionally (but mostly when he's feeling particularly profound or uncomfortable.)

Unprofessionally, he also speaks occasionally (but mostly when he's tipsy and in the mood to give a toast.)

---

[8] You may have noticed at the start of the book I said I'd decided it was time to quit my job and move to Silicon Valley. I get to be a living example of life's curveballs. The tech dream I followed took me elsewhere. (The tacos are better here anyway, don't @ me.)